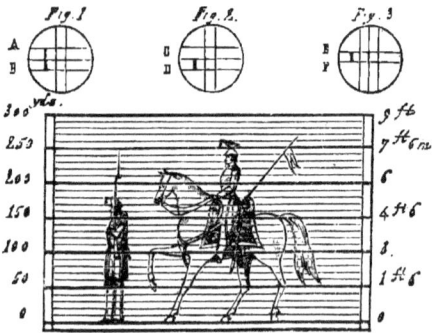

Fig. 1   Fig. 2.   Fig. 3

A
B

C
D

E
F

300 yds.   9 ft
250   7 ft 6 in.
200   6
150   4 ft 6
100   3.
50   1 ft 6
0   0

THE

SOLDIER'S MANUAL

OF

RIFLE FIRING,

AT VARIOUS DISTANCES.

THE

SOLDIER'S MANUAL

OF

RIFLE FIRING,

AT VARIOUS DISTANCES.

BY

CAPTAIN THACKERAY,

2nd SOMERSET MILITIA,

AUTHOR OF THREE LECTURES ON THE PRACTICE OF
RIFLE FIRING &c., &c.

The Naval & Military Press Ltd

Published by

The Naval & Military Press Ltd

Unit 5 Riverside, Brambleside
Bellbrook Industrial Estate
Uckfield, East Sussex
TN22 1QQ England

Tel: +44 (0)1825 749494

www.naval-military-press.com
www.nmarchive.com

TO THE BRITISH ARMY

THIS ESSAY

IS DEDICATED BY

THE AUTHOR.

INTRODUCTION.

BEFORE entering more particularly on the subject of this treatise, it may not be without interest to give some brief history of the various inventions of portable arms for the projection of offensive missiles, which have at length produced the Rifle, in its present comparatively perfect state.

Arms of projection occupied but a secondary place in ancient warfare. The sling, and some others for the projection of stones, the bow and the cross-bow for the projection of arrows, were among the rude weapons of times preceding the 14th century.

The arquebus, a later invention, supplied a transition as it were between these and the more modern arms in which the projectile force is derived from gunpowder. This implement was formed of a tube, from which leaden balls were thrown by means of a cord suddenly released from a powerful spring.

The invention of powder occasioned a complete revolution, not only in the art of war, but in warlike weapons.

The first portable fire-arms were made in the 14th century. The ancient arquebus supplied the primitive idea of these arms. The tube or barrel from which the ball or projectile issues is still preserved, the projectile force of the cord being superseded by that of gunpowder.

The first kind of fire-arms were a species of small cannon borne by two men. They were fired from a rest by a lighted match; to these succeeded the Culverine, so called from its being principally constructed of brass or bronze, a more manageable implement, although still very rude and imperfect.

This, about 1480, was followed by the Petronel, or Poitrinal, which derived its name from being supported on the chest or poitrine (the French term for the chest) of the person using it; this was also often called an Arquebus.

The frequent wars of the 14th and 15th centuries, caused a very rapid extension in the use of the fire-arms of those times. In 1364, about 500 fire-arms were manufactured at Perugia. In 1404, at a review of the army at Padua, a considerable number of men were armed with hand cannon and arquebuses.

In 1414, the Burgundians, who defended the city of Arras against Charles V., had fire-arms from which were thrown leaden balls.

The Swedes made use of fire-arms in the 14th century, and in 1431, the city of Stockholm had its Arquebusiers.

In 1449, Piccignini and Gonzagues left Milan with 20,000 men, armed with arquebuses, to raise the siege of Marignan.

At the battle of Morat, in 1476, the Swiss, in their army of 31,000 men, reckoned 10,000 men armed with fire-arms.

The first fire-arms were discharged by a lighted match applied by the hand, but towards the close of the 14th century, this was replaced for portable fire-arms, by a mechanical contrivance, although very rude and inconvenient, called a serpentine, by which the match was brought into contact with the powder; but, to avoid accident, this match was extinguished during the operation of loading, and lighted after that operation was complete; so that little was gained by the invention.

A considerable advance was, however, made in 1517, by the invention at Nurembourgh, of the wheel, or German lock. This was a small wheel of steel, which was made to revolve quickly in connexion with a piece of metal being an alloy of antimony and iron, and by the friction occasioned by this rapid movement, disengaged sparks of fire, by which the powder was ignited.

This was afterwards replaced by a rude flint lock, at a later part of this same century.

About 1521, the Musket, which was a modification of the Petronel or Arquebus, in which the butt or stock was supported on the right side of the chest or shoulder, whilst the other end rested on a portable support or rest, was introduced, and was employed for the first time in that year in the army of Charles V. From this time to the commencement of the 17th century, considerable extension was given to the use of this weapon, and at that period the infantry were almost universally composed of musqueteers and pikemen, the former as their names import, armed with muskets, the latter with pikes.

The first muskets were very heavy, and threw balls of eight or ten to the pound weight, to considerable distances; but their inconvenience being greater than their utility, they were gradually reduced in length and calibre, or bore, until they were rendered tolerably easily portable, and could be fired from the shoulder.

From the Musket the gradation to the Rifle,—from the rude flint to the percussion lock, has continued from time to time, until we have been furnished with the almost perfect weapon we now possess.

We cannot pass over in complete silence some of the later inventions, which have contributed so much to the efficiency of the Infantry, by furnishing them with weapons that leave at an immeasurable distance the old musket.

Since 1840, various and important has been the progress of invention. In that year a new form of Rifle, possessing considerable advantages, was adopted in France. This was followed in 1842, by a Rifle, much improved, by Captain Delvigne, of the French army; and this again was succeeded by the well known " Minié Rifle à tige,"—so named from the particular form of a ball invented by Captain Minié, who also belongs to the French army. Our transatlantic brethren, the Americans, have not been behind hand in the race of invention; and some of them have, as is well known here, been lately exhibiting a "breech loading and self-cleaning Rifle," which is very favourably reported of. The Prussian needle-gun is another form of Rifle, which is stated to possess peculiar merit; and a modification of this by one of our own makers, Mr. Needham, of Piccadilly, lays claim to great consideration. In this Rifle capping and cocking are entirely dispensed with; and it can, it is asserted, be loaded and fired twelve times in a minute, and will shoot with great precision.

There is another important invention by Lancaster, of London, which may be termed an anomaly in gun making, and which he calls his Patent Smooth-bored Rifle. It is elliptical, and not cylindrical in its bore; and from experiments made at Woolwich, before competent authorities, the following results were obtained:—

> At 500 yards, 2 out of 4 shots hit the bull's eye,
> At 400 yards, 2 out of 3 shots hit the bull's eye,
> At 200 yards, 6 shots fired all round the bull's eye.

From experiments made the same day upon the Minié or French Rifle, the following results were obtained:—

> At 500 yards, 1 out of 4 shots hit the bull's eye,
> At 400 yards, 1 out of 3 shots hit the bull's eye,
> At 200 yards, the whole six struck the target,

giving on these experiments a vast superiority in favour of Lancaster's invention over the Minié or French Rifle.

The improvements recently introduced in Rifles, have obtained for these weapons a degree of range and precision, of which but a few years since, no one would have considered them susceptible.

These qualities, and the general introduction into the army of the Rifle, must, of necessity, give an importance to the infantry superior to any they have hitherto attained, and will modify considerably any operations in which they may be hereafter engaged. Instead of being placed as formerly at a distance comparatively near to an enemy, great advantages will result in their being employed at distances of 5 or 600 yards, or even more. Instead of always acting in large bodies, some of their most efficient services will be rendered in small detachments. The fire of the infantry being much more effective, and at greater distances, their value in the field, in comparison with cavalry and artillery, will be very materially augmented.

The cavalry will be exposed to their destructive fire, without the possibility, from their distance, of checking it; and a few expert shots, well stationed, and availing themselves of the cover afforded by the accidental formation of the ground, will be able to silence artillery, by picking off the men, and to render it inefficient by disabling the horses, without affording any chance of being harmed by the guns; and even should they be unable to obtain cover, the mark that would be afforded by detached and single men would be so small, and the distance so considerable, that artillery would have but a very unequal chance. Added to this, the infantry soldier could fire eight or ten times to one, to a large gun; and thus might one man clear every gun of its men, for one shot fired against him. Cavalry and artillery would thus lose much of their comparative value in the field.

This view of the matter, however, is dependent on the supposition that the infantry render themselves as efficient in the use of the Rifle, as the Rifle is efficient from its present improvement.

CONTENTS.

CHAPTER I.

CHAPTER II.

CHAPTER III.

CHAPTER IV.

CHAPTER V.

CHAPTER VI.

MANUAL OF RIFLE FIRING.

THE object of this Treatise is to afford the soldier such information on rifle firing as shall, if carried out in practice, make
him efficient in that branch of his duty. With a view to this,
a plain manner and language will be adopted, with as little use
of scientific terms or descriptions as possible, so as to bring
within the intelligence of every reader the means of clearly com-
prehending the subject.

We purpose treating the matter before us so as to be not only
easily intelligible, but from the simplicity of its arrangement so
to impress itself on the mind as to be made readily available for
actual service.

We shall begin by giving the soldier some general directions,
and shall afterwards afford him all the information that may
appear to us to be essential to his perfection in rifle firing, following the order and subject of such directions.

We therefore propose that,—

First. The soldier should make himself perfectly acquainted
with his rifle, its different parts, and the accoutrements belong-
ing to it. He should be able to take it to pieces, to put it together, and to keep it perfectly clean; and to this latter point he
should pay particular attention, since something of his success
as a marksman depends on it.

Secondly. He should know what is the exact charge, and if
need be, be able to make his own cartridges, cast his own balls,
&c.

Thirdly. He should know the theory of taking aim and firing, and the entire management of his rifle for these purposes; and should, by incessant practice, render himself an expert marksman and an able shot.

Fourthly. He should be able correctly to estimate distances by sight, and without the aid of instruments.

Fifthly. He should know, so as to be able to apply his knowledge at the instant, at what part of an object to aim, at any given distance.

Sixthly. He should be able, from practice and observation, to remedy any defects in the firing of his rifle, and to make allowances for deviations of the ball, in reference to the several causes producing them.

CHAPTER I.

THE RIFLE.

THE Rifle consists of six principal parts—

1 The barrel,   4 The ramrod,
2 The lock,   5 The bayonet,
3 The butt or stock,   6 The fittings.

1 The Barrel.

The barrel receives the charge, resists the explosion of the powder, and directs the ball.

The barrel consists of

1 The mouth or muzzle,   3 The breech,
2 The interior which is rifled,   4 The sights.

2 The Lock.

The lock consists of
1 The cock,   3 The internal mechanism.
2 The nipple,

3 The Butt or Stock

receives the barrel, the lock, and the ramrod, and is fitted with a trigger-guard.

4 The Ramrod,
5 The Bayonet,
6 The Fittings,

require no particular explanation.

The Armourer in each Regiment will more particularly describe to the men the various parts of the Rifle, and will instruct them in the taking it to pieces and putting it together, and give them particular directions as to cleaning it. It may, however, be well to give some general hints as to the cleaning, which may be useful to the soldier when the Armourer cannot be consulted.

To preserve the Rifle from rust, it should be rubbed over occasionally with a piece of soft rag and a little of the grease, of which we will presently give directions as to the making. The same course will be taken with the bayonet and ramrod.

The washing the barrel is attended with more difficulty than in the case of the common musket. A particular kind of washing-rod is provided for this purpose, on which a piece of rag being placed it should be pushed into the barrel, at the same time moving the barrel to and fro from left to right. Care should be taken that the barrel is thoroughly dried after washing, and that no particles of the rag are left in the rifled parts of the barrel. The want of this latter precaution may occasion the rifle to miss fire, and be the cause of serious accident.

After washing and drying, the barrel of the Rifle should be rubbed inside with oiled rag, and the oil thus deposited should be left on the Rifle until it is wanted for use, when it should be cleaned out with a piece of dry rag; and if practicable, should before used be flashed off with loose powder, to shew that it is fit for service.

After the Rifle is cleaned, the cock should be carefully let down on the nipple, where it should remain when the Rifle is not used for firing.

It sometimes happens that it is necessary to draw the charge. In this case the cap should be removed from the nipple, and the nipple carefully cleaned from any of the detonating powder that may be left on it, to avoid the chance of accident.

Manner of Preparing the Grease.

Take a pound of olive oil, of good quality, and half a pound of mutton suet; melt the suet alone over a slow fire, and whilst hot, strain it through a coarse cloth. Mix the oil and suet while warm. This will make a kind of pomatum, which must be kept free from dust or dirt.

Blacking for the Leather Appendages.

	lbs.
Yellow wax	3
White wax	1
Spirit of turpentine	7½
Ivory black	1
Colophone, a kind of black resin used to give a bright polish	⅛

This will make about 12 lbs., a quantity sufficient for the use of a company for a year.

The manner of preparing the blacking is as follows :—Scrape the wax, put it in a vessel, and pour over it enough spirit of turpentine to cover it. Pound the colophone, and put it in another vessel, and cover it also with spirit of turpentine.

Cover the two vessels close, so that the spirit shall not evaporate, and let them remain 24 hours. At the end of that time mix the contents of the two vessels, add the ivory black, and stir with a stick, pouring in the rest of the spirit slowly until the whole is well mixed. This makes a kind of ointment that is easily applied.

In using it, rub a small quantity over the leather, and, having left it for about half an hour, then rub it with a soft cloth until a fine polish is obtained.

CHAPTER II.

THE CHARGE. MAKING CARTRIDGES. CASTING BALLS.

THE charge for the soldier's Rifle is decided on by the proper military authorities, and may easily be ascertained by inquiry of the proper officer in each regiment, who will also instruct the soldier in making cartridges and casting balls, as regards which it would be somewhat difficult to convey such information as would be intelligible other than by practical means.

It may, however, be useful to point out that in casting balls the melted lead is in a proper state when it burns a piece of paper that is plunged into it.

In order, also, to keep the melted lead in a fit state, a layer of powdered charcoal of about an eighth of an inch thick should be placed on it in the melting pot.

CHAPTER III.

TAKING AIM AND FIRING.

THE general principles of taking aim and firing applicable to all fire-arms, are founded on the relative positions existing between three imaginary lines :

1 The line of projection;   2 The trajectory;
3 The line of vision.

POINT BLANK RANGE

LINE OF PROJECTION

TRAJECTORY

LINE OF VISION

Fig 1

These lines are shown in fig. 1.

The line of projection is a right or straight line drawn through the axis or centre of the barrel of the rifle lengthways, and extending beyond the barrel to any supposed length.

The trajectory is a curved or bent line followed or taken by the ball in its progress through the air from the rifle to the object.

The line of vision is a right or straight line passing through the centre of the back sight on the rifle and the centre of the front sight near the muzzle of the rifle to the object.

Now in order to the certain understanding of these lines, after having studied them in fig. 1, lay a rifle down on a table, and with a piece of chalk, draw a straight line on the table from the centre lengthways of the barrel—this will be the line of projection.

Draw another straight line through the sights—this will be the line of vision.

Draw another curved or bent line beginning in the same direction with the line of projection and afterwards crossing the line of vision at two points, as shewn in fig. 1—this will be the trajectory.

It is absolutely necessary, before going further, to study these lines, in order thoroughly to understand them, for a correct knowledge of them lies at the very foundation of good rifle firing.

It may be as well here to explain the principles affecting the passage of the ball from the rifle, by which the reason of the curve forming the trajectory will be readily understood.

A projectile—a ball for example—thrown in any given direction by any force, as for instance, the force of powder exploded

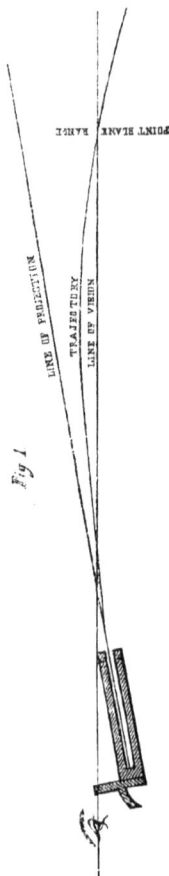

in a Rifle, would, by virtue of the law of inertia, or the indisposition of matter to change its state of rest or motion, continue always to proceed in the same direction with the same velocity, if it did not suffer or meet with some opposing force or resistance in a direction differing from that first given to it. Now, in the case of a ball fired from a rifle, there are two opposing forces. First, the attraction of gravitation to the earth's centre; secondly, the resistance of the atmosphere or air, the former drawing the ball continually towards the earth, and the latter diminishing continually its velocity. On the ball first issuing from the rifle, the velocity imparted to it by the powder is so great, that it almost wholly overcomes the two opposing forces, and therefore proceeds nearly in a straight or right line with the axis of the barrel, or in other words, with the line of projection; but as it proceeds, these two resisting forces come into more powerful operation, and as the velocity is diminished by the resistance of the atmosphere or air, the attraction of gravitation increases in intensity, or operates more powerfully. Instead, therefore, of proceeding in a straight line, the ball thus acted upon, and continually drawn downwards, after crossing near the muzzle the line of vision, is compelled to travel in a curve : this curve, or the course described by the projectile in its passage through the air, is called the trajectory.

There is another and very simple manner of shewing the principle of the trajectory which is familiar to every one—the common act of throwing a stone. We know that if we throw a stone, it has a tendency from the moment it leaves the hand, to fall to the earth; and we therefore, if we wish to strike an object beyond a certain distance, throw the stone higher into the air, in order that it may not reach the earth at a point nearer to us than the object. The stone, in the same manner as the ball fired from the rifle, forms a curved line from the moment that the force given to it by the hand ceases to be sufficient to overcome the effect of the attraction of gravitation.

This curved line is in effect the trajectory. The stone may be considered as the rifle ball, and the hand as the rifle. The point where the trajectory the second time crosses the line of

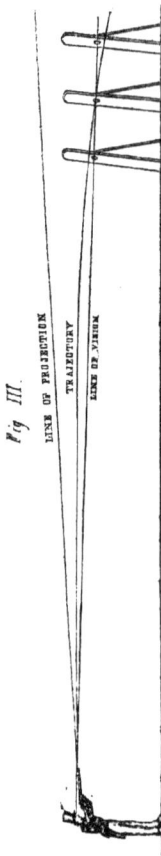

vision (figs. I., III.) is called the point-blank range, which should be the centre of the object to be struck.

We shall now explain some other points necessary to be understood.

The space that is between two straight lines which meet each other at the point where they join, is called an angle thus—

A is a vertical line, and B a horizontal line.

Now if a piece of cardboard be placed upright, it will be a vertical plane. If it be placed on a flat surface, it becomes and is a horizontal plane.

The two straight lines—B and C—meeting each other at A form an angle at A.

A plane being a simple idea, is difficult to describe in common language, but will probably be understood if we say that it is a level surface, like for example a sheet of cardboard or a deal plank.

Vertical means in common language, upright; horizontal means in the same language, lying flat; thus—

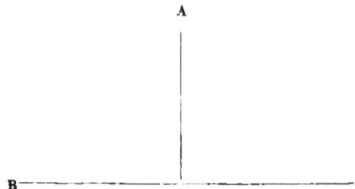

The angle of projection is the angle that the line of projection forms with the horizon, or popularly speaking, with the visible surface of the earth at the moment of firing.

The angle of vision is the angle formed by the line of vision with the line of projection.

A plane which is vertical, and contains the line of projection at the moment of firing, is called the plane of projection.

The trajectory is wholly in this plane. It is at first coincident, or similar to the line of projection, but afterwards diverges or deviates from it, more and more, as the ball's distance from the muzzle of the rifle is increased.

When the line of vision is horizontal, and placed in the plane of projection, the angle of vision is equal to the angle of projection.

The trajectory and the line of vision may be considered as invariably related, when the latter of these lines is in the plane of projection.

In this case, if the line of vision be raised or depressed, or be directed to the right or left, the trajectory participates in these different movements, and always preserves in all its parts the same position relatively to the line of vision, provided that too great an inclination above or below the horizon be not given to it.

Since the trajectory is contained in the plane of projection, if care be taken to place the line of vision in this plane, and to direct this line on the vertical passing through the point to be attained, the ball will touch in some part the vertical in question, if such line be not without the limits of the range. In order that this point of contact shall be precisely the object to be struck, it only remains to direct the line of vision, or what is the same, the visual ray passing along the bottom of the notch or the sight and the top of the guide, on such a point of the vertical that the trajectory should cut the object.

The point in question will be determined when it is known how much the trajectory rises above, or descends below the line of vision, at the distance between the object and the muzzle of the rifle.

If, for example, it be known that the trajectory, at a certain distance, descends a yard below the line of vision, it will be necessary, in order to strike an object situate at such distance, to direct the line of vision, or, in other words, to take aim a yard above such object. For if the line of vision were directed, or aim were taken, exactly to such object, the ball or trajectory

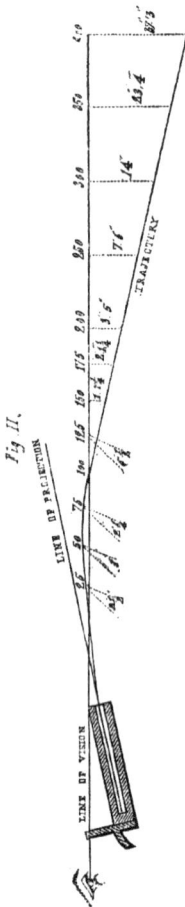

would pass a yard below it, as shewn in Fig. II. But if the line of vision be directed, or aim be taken, a yard above the object, the trajectory will follow the movement of the line of vision; will preserve, with reference to this, its first position; and will, consequently, pass a yard below the point sighted—that is, will exactly meet the object.

It must be kept in mind that the line of vision is placed in the plane of projection, when at the moment of firing, the notch of the back-sight and the top of the sight near the muzzle of the barrel are not inclined either to the right or left of a vertical plane leading to the eye, and passing by the middle of the barrel lengthways; and care must, therefore, be taken to hold the Rifle so that the sight is directly vertical, or in popular language upright.

The firing of the Rifle can then be regulated by means of the line of vision, when the position of different points of the trajectory relatively to this right line is known, and when care is taken to place the two points, which determine the line of vision in the plane of projection.

If the trajectory and the line of vision, in the position which they generally occupy with relation to each other, be examined, it will be observed that the line of vision cuts or intersects the trajectory at two points, one very near the muzzle of the Rifle, and the other at a greater distance.

The second point of intersection of the trajectory and the line of vision, is called the point-blank range, as has before been stated.

To each line of vision a special point-blank range corresponds.

The point-blank range is increased in proportion as the notch or opening of the sight of the Rifle is raised, or the requisite elevation is given.

It will be observed (Fig. II.), that beyond the point-blank range the trajectory descends below the line of vision, and the more so as the ball's distance from the Rifle is increased.

That within the point-blank range, between the two points of intersection of the line of vision and the trajectory, the ball rises above the line of vision in different degrees according to the position under consideration.

That the elevation of the ball is very small near the points of intersection, and greater towards the middle of the right line, or line of vision, which joins these two points.

That from the muzzle of the Rifle to the first intersection, the centre of the ball is below the line of vision in different degrees, according to the point from which the centre of the ball is considered or taken ; but these degrees are all very small, so that in this part of its course the ball may be regarded practically as being on the line of vision.

Since at a distance equal to the point-blank range the trajectory meets the line of vision, it will be sufficient to direct the line of vision on such point to strike an object situated at that distance.

Since beyond the point-blank range the trajectory descends below the line of vision, it will be necessary, in order to strike an object situate at a greater distance than the point-blank range, to direct the line of aim above the object, for if it were directed straight to the object, the trajectory would pass below it.

To determine the elevation of the sight to be taken so as to strike the object, it is only necessary to know the descent of the trajectory below the line of vision at the distance at which the object to be struck is placed. This descent is equal to the elevation that should be taken above the object. This will be evident when it is remembered that the trajectory is relatively connected with the line of vision.

It will be equally clear that to strike an object situate between the two intersections of the line of vision and the trajectory, a sight must be taken below the object at a point vertically distant from the first or line of vision, of a length equal to that which separates the trajectory from the line of vision at the distance at which the object to be struck is placed.

It must be observed that to strike an object at the same distance from the muzzle of the Rifle, as the first intersection of the line of vision and the trajectory, the object must be aimed at directly.

Such are the general conditions for firing, which may be reduced to the general following rules :—

When the object is situate at one of the points of intersection of the trajectory and the line of vision, the object itself must be aimed at.

When the object is situate between the two points of intersection, an aim must be taken below the object.

When the object is situate beyond the point-blank range, or the second point of intersection of the line of vision and the trajectory, an aim must be taken above the object, and the further the object is removed, the higher must be relatively the aim.

When the object is situate between the muzzle of the Rifle and the first point of intersection, an aim must be taken above the object.

These general principles being well understood, the next point will be to reduce them to practice.

Since sights on the Rifle are provided so as to indicate th range, or in other words the point blank, where the trajecto the second time cuts or crosses the line of vision, the foregoir observations are intended chiefly for the information of thᴇ soldier on the theory of Rifle firing rather than for any practical necessity, and the same reason will render useless our entering here into any mathematical calculations to determine the point-blank range for given distances. No other operation will be required on the part of the soldier, than merely regulating the sight corresponding with the distance, as shewn by the graduated scale of the sight.

The explanation of this graduated scale, and the means of adapting it, will lie with the instructor, by whom a very short tuition will render the soldier thoroughly competent on this point.

The first part of the instruction of Rifle firing may commence in the barrack room or yards, and should consist in the instructor pointing out to each man individually the nature of the sights on the Rifle, their use as affecting the range, the mode of shifting them, and how to point and level the Rifle at all distances.

The soldier's first practice will be accurately to take aim,—for this purpose a *traversing rest* should be provided ; this is a piece of wood scooped out to receive the Rifle, placed on a stand, and capable of being elevated, depressed, or made to traverse or turn at will ; or in the absence of this, an ordinary sand bag may be placed on the barrack table or window sill. On this rest, or sand bag, the soldier should place his Rifle, and take an aim, using the sight appropriated to some given distance;—the best object for this practice will be a straight rod placed quite upright.

Having taken aim, the soldier should leave his Rifle on the rest, which should be examined by the instructor to ascertain that the sight is properly adapted, that the front and back sights, and the object exactly cover each other, and that the aim is perfectly true.

When the aim is ascertained by the instructor to be correct, he should fold down the elevating or back sight on the barrel, desiring the man to look again along the barrel, in order that he may form an idea of the amount of elevation that was required to attain the range named.

The instructor should also see that the sight, and back sight, are perfectly vertical or upright, and not inclining either to the right or left, since, if they should so incline to the right or to the 'eft, the trajectory and line of vision will not lie in the same ertical or upright plane, and consequently will not intersect ach other, and the ball will consequently not strike the object 'med at. It seems to be understood, at least in the lower ranges 'larked on the scale of the sights, that either an elevation or depression of two feet on the face of the target, will make a difference of about thirty yards in the extent of range.

This practice should be continued for a sufficient length of time to render the soldier perfectly conversant with the various sights, and competent to take aim correctly. When this shall have been accomplished, the soldier must go through the same exercise with the Rifle held to his shoulder, instead of being placed on a rest.

For this purpose he must be carefully taught by the instructor the mode of holding the Rifle, so as to ensure its being quite steady; and the mode of pressing the trigger, so as not to occasion any change of position of the Rifle in firing.

The Rifle should be held by the left hand, placed so far forward as not to occasion any inconvenience in the posture—since the further the hand is extended the more equal will be the comparative leverage or balance of the Rifle on either side of the hand, and the greater will be the facility of holding it perfectly steady. A pressure towards the shoulder will be exerted by the left hand, which will also contribute to the steadying of the Rifle. The right hand will hold the Rifle clasping it below the trigger guard, and will press the butt firmly to the shoulder, being assisted in steadying the Rifle by the inner and lower part of the right arm. The first or trigger finger must be placed lightly on the trigger, so that in firing, its only motion will be very gradually to press the trigger without the slightest jerk, since if it be placed at any distance from the trigger, the movement towards the trigger for the purpose of pulling it, will most probably cause a deviation in the direction of the Rifle. The second joint of the first finger should be placed on the trigger, and used to pull it; and the trigger must be pressed by the finger without any jerk or movement of the elbow.

A very important point to observe is, that from the moment of finally taking aim until after the firing, the breathing should be stopped, so that the motion of the chest in taking breath do not change the position of the Rifle.

For the purpose of taking aim the head should be inclined, or leaned down a little to the right, so as to bring the right eye immediately over the tangent or back sight, and in a line with the sight at the muzzle or the barrel. Aim must be taken with the right eye, the left eye being closed.

In order to enable the instructor to determine the precision of aim by the soldier, during this process of preliminary instruction of firing from the shoulder, the instructor placing himself about ten or twelve yards in front of the soldier, and telling him to aim at his right eye, will be able to ascertain if the soldier has acquired the necessary requisites for aiming correctly.

The next point will be to practise the soldier in taking aim at an object at any assigned distance, and as to this the duties of the instructor must necessarily be confined to seeing that the proper sights are used, that the rifle is held in the proper position, and that the trigger finger is so placed and used, as not to cause a deviation from the line of aim.

The sights are graduated or marked with various distances, from 200 up to 1000 yards. The first and last of these are fixed and immovable, but the others are regulated by means of a sliding bar, which may be placed at pleasure at any intermediate distance between 400 and 1000 yards.

In directing the rifle at any object, therefore, less than 200 yards, if the sight for 200 yards be used, it will be necessary to make allowance for the difference, and to aim proportionably below the object; and so if the 400 yard sight should be used for an object at less than that distance. But if the 200 yard sight be used for an object beyond that distance, an aim proportionably above the object must be taken, and so for the 400 yard sight, if it be used for an object beyond it.

The other sights will necessarily be adjusted by the sliding bar accurately, with respect to the exact distance of the object.

The point of an object at which aim should be taken, if it be at point-blank range, is the centre—if it be near, but within point-blank range, the lower part—and, if near, but without point-blank range, the upper part.

In this first part of the practice of firing from the shoulder, the trigger is of course to be pulled so that the cock will fall; but in this case, precaution must be taken by placing a small piece of leather, or India-rubber, around the nipple, that the cock be not broken in falling on the nipple, in the absence of the cap.

The next course of practice will be with caps, which will in most points be but a repetition of the preceding ; but in order to ascertain that the men aim correctly, a lighted candle may be placed at some short distance from the muzzle of the rifle, which, in the event of the aim being precise, will generally be extinguished. This practice, as far as relates to firing at the lighted candle, must be confined to aim taken with the 200 yard sight.

This will be followed by firing with blank cartridge, and subsequently with ball.

In ball firing, care must be taken by the officer, that, so far as he can control it, no portion of the powder in the cartridge should be lost; and the men must, therefore, be charged to be particularly careful in biting off the end of the cartridge, not to suffer any portion of the powder to be wasted, since all difference in the quantity of powder will make a corresponding difference in the range of the rifle; the cartridges being carefully prepared in relation to the sights on the rifles.

In ball firing, the soldier must begin to aim below the object to be hit, by gradually raising the muzzle of the rifle in a straight line up to the object (or bull's-eye), and at that instant the trigger should be pressed, and the piece discharged—for the following reason :—As long as you preserve the vertical or upright motion, no lateral motion can take place ; but if your aim was taken at the object to be struck for any length of time, say a few seconds only, your Musket or Rifle would be forming a circle around the object to be struck.

In the first period of ball practice, it would be well to place a target of eight feet diameter at a short distance, say fifty yards, in order to give confidence to the men, and to detect more easily their incompetence in taking precise aim ; and it would be advisable to continue the practice with this target, until they have acquired a certain proficiency.

Such of them as shall fail to any considerable extent in firing

Fig III

LINE OF PROJECTION

TRAJECTORY

LINE OF VISION

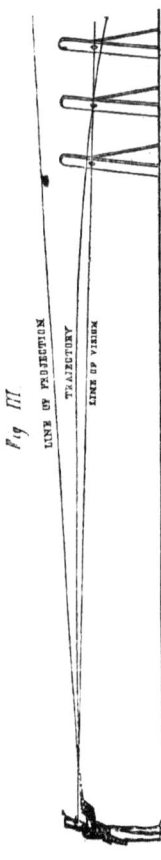

with tolerable accuracy, should not be permitted to continue ball practice, but should go back to the drill of aiming, and not be allowed to resume the ball firing until they should have proved themselves more competent.

Such as shall succeed to any fair extent may be formed into separate squads or classes, according to merit.

This will excite emulation among the men by a desire to be ranked in the higher classes, and by finding in their respective classes competitors of equal skill with themselves.

Prizes may also with good effect be given to the most able at stated periods.

This practice may be varied by the men firing sometimes from the knee, and sometimes standing.

After the men have shewn a tolerable proficiency in firing at this first target, it would be well to place a second target at a certain distance— say 30 or 40 yards behind it, as in fig. III. The ball, having passed through the first target, would then pass through the second target at a higher or lower point, and would thus afford a means of shewing practically, and explaining to the men, the line of projection, the trajectory, and the line of vision.

So soon as the firing at this first target should have acquired something like perfection, the distance may be increased, and targets of the ordinary dimensions of 6 feet by 2 may

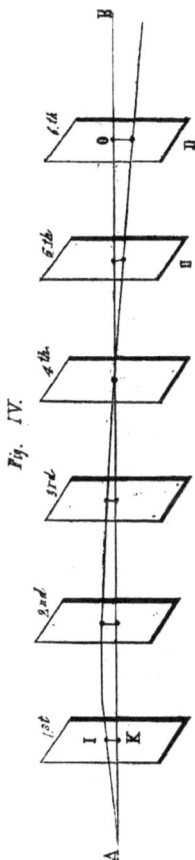

Fig. IV.

be used: they should be painted
black or white, according to the
colour of the objects opposed to
them, with a white or black spot, or
bull's-eye of 6 inches in diameter,
in the centre. They should be divided into three squares by two
horizontal lines. These divisions
are called the upper, the centre, and
lower divisions of the target.

Up to 225 yards, the practice will
be at a single target.

From 225 to 300, at two,
From 325 to 400, at three,
From 425 to 500, at four,
From 600   at five,
From 700   at six,
From 800   at eight targets.

The targets being placed very near
together.

It may be observed, that the
ranges are marked on the scale of
the sight, in the supposition that the
sights have in every instance been
placed with perfect accuracy, but the
soldier will be prepared to discover
some peculiarity in his own musket
or rifle, for which allowance must
be made, and must not be discou-
raged if even, having found a means
of remedying its defects, he does not
always hit the mark, or make equally
good practice. There are various
causes, which will be more particularly detailed hereafter, which may
operate against him, but for which,
when he becomes sufficiently expe-
rienced, he will be able to make due
allowance, so as to reduce or coun-
teract their effects.

If from these, or any other causes, he should not arrive at perfection so soon as he may desire, or should be detained, or even sent back by his commanding officer to the preliminary practice of learning to aim, he may be perfectly convinced that his own interests demand such a course, even more imperiously than the interests of the service ; since a soldier may not unfrequently be placed in circumstances where his skill, and that coolness which is the consequence of confidence in his skill, may be the means of acquiring to him honour and promotion.

CHAPTER IV.

ESTIMATION OF DISTANCES.

WE have considered the principles and practice of firing; but it will easily be conceived that how important soever these may be, and certainly are, the just appreciation or estimation of distances at which the object fired at may be, is of equal or even of greater importance. It is impossible, indeed, to bring into effect the rules we have laid down, if the soldier cannot pretty accurately judge of the distance of the object which he has to strike, the rules for firing at such or such a distance, having reference only to the prescribed distance.

Continued trials and frequent observation can alone confer a habit of judging of distances, and that readiness and quickness in deciding on them, which are absolutely essential to make an expert marksman.

In firing at the target, or otherwise simply for practice, the distances are measured and well known, and nothing is required but to aim correctly, and to fire with care and attention to the rules prescribed ; but when the soldier is opposed to an enemy, the distance is necessarily unknown, and it is absolutely essential to decide with promptitude, and as exactly as possible the distance, and to regulate the firing accordingly.

The estimation of distances is made either by simply judging of them by sight, or by the aid of instruments.

We shall first consider the means of acquiring facility of judging of distances simply by sight.

A distance, say of 200 yards, will be measured off by a chain, and divided by some marks, such as small sticks stuck in the ground, small stones, or scratches made in the ground, into distances of 50, 100, 150, and 200 yards. The men will then be made to pace this ground so marked, stepping in their ordinary manner, without increasing or lessening their usual mode of stepping. They will be directed to count the number of paces in each 50 yards, and to continue this until they shall have attained an equal number of paces in each 50 yards. They will take the same course as to 100 yards.

When this shall have been accomplished, they will begin again at the commencement of the 200 yards, and pace over the whole distance, until they shall be able to pace the 200 yards in double the number of paces they took for 100 yards.

When they shall be proficient in this, they will leave the ground that has been measured off, and go to another ground, and there pace 25, 50, 100, 150, and 200 yards, until they shall have acquired a complete facility in pacing any distance within 200 yards. They will mark the distances they pace on this unmeasured ground, and they will be checked by being measured with the chain by the instructor; and this exercise they will continue until they are quite competent to pace any assigned distance, less than 200 yards, correctly.

In all these exercises there must be placed at the point from which the soldier departs, some mark sufficiently conspicuous to be seen by him after he has paced the several distances, so as to enable him, on turning round, to observe his distance from such point.

This having been accomplished, the instructor will form his detachment in rank at that end of the 200 yards at which the measuring was commenced, so that the measured line shall be perpendicular to the front of the detachment, one end being at the middle of the line. He will order four men of the detachment to go, one to 50 yards, another to 100 yards, another to 150 yards, and the other to 200 yards, and to front the company.

He should order on this service men of the ordinary height and size, who have no peculiarity of dress, nor any thing to attract particular attention. These men should carry their ordinary arms and equipments. The instructor should cause the men, placed in rank, to observe the various parts of each of the men, his dress, arms, and equipments, and point out to them that such of these, as are distinctly visible at 50 yards, are either not so clearly visible, or are reduced in apparent size, at 100 yards; that they are still less clearly visible, or more apparently reduced, at 150 yards; and so on.

He will then ask each man separately what are his observations on these several points, and will explain to him the effects produced to the eye by objects viewed at different distances; thus it is pointed out to him, that, at 50 yards the features of the man, the buttons on his jacket, the band and star on his foraging cap, can be plainly recognized, while at 100 yards the lineaments can no longer be discerned, the buttons seem to form a continuous line, the star is scarcely separable from the band, and at 150 yards the buttons are quite invisible, and the face looks like a whitish ball under the line of the cap.

.It will be indispensable that he shall point out to the men, that in foggy or cloudy weather, objects having much less light falling on them, appear much more distant than they really are, and that in clear sunshiny days, being much more lighted, the details are much more easily visible, and the object appears nearer than it is in reality. In an avenue of trees, objects appear from the effects of perspective much more distant than they really are ; and the absence or contiguity of other objects, and the effects of light and shade, may apparently increase or diminish the distance in many cases.

When the men shall have been sufficiently drilled in this estimation of distance, the instructor will change their position to some unmeasured ground, and send a soldier armed and equipped as before, and as near as may be of the same height and figure as one of the four men already employed, to some distance which shall be determined by desiring him to halt. At this distance he is to turn and face the company ; the instructor will then command the men in rank to observe the man so sent out, and to estimate his distance, bearing in mind the observations they have already made on the four men, placed previously at certain known distances.

Having done this, he will call each man separately out of the ranks, and, making him speak in a low tone of voice, he will question him as to the distance, and as to his reasons for the opinion that he has formed ; and the instructor will make a note of the distance assigned by each soldier.

The instructor will then cause each man to pace the distance, and will take a note of each man's measurement, and he will finally verify the measurement by the chain.

After this verification, the instructor will read the statement of each of the men aloud, and will make such observations on them to the men generally, as will lead to a more just estimate of the distance on any future trial.

The instructor must repeat this exercise continually until the men can pretty accurately judge of all distances not exceeding 200 yards; taking for each exercise a different ground, having, if possible, a difference of surrounding objects and colours, and a different conformation. These drills should also take place in different states of the atmosphere; at various parts of the day, morning and evening, and with different effects of light and shade. They should also be made with the sun in front, and behind the men, and in other positions as regards the sun.

In these drills also selections may be made of the most competent men; and they may be formed into various classes, according to merit.

When the instructor shall consider that his men know how to estimate, with sufficient accuracy, the distances included within 200 yards, he will proceed to the estimation of distances between 200 yards and 400 yards. With this view, he will measure with the chain a distance of 400 yards, and mark on the measured line distances of 200, 250, 300, 350, and 400 yards. The detachment being in line, he will order five men to take up positions as before, at each of these distances, the first at 200 yards, the second at 250 yards, and so on, and then to face the line.

He will then go through the same course as he already did for the previous distances; but in this case, the measured point of 200 yards will be the term of comparison for the longer distances. When the men are sufficiently capable of thus judging of these greater distances by the five men so placed, the instructor will take the same means by sending only one man to some uncertain distance, at which he will be made to halt as before, and precisely the same means will be taken to perfect the men in judging of the longer distances up to 400 yards.

After 400 yards, the distances will no longer be marked by single men sent out to certain distances, but by detachments. The distances up to 900 or 1000 yards, will be measured in the first instance as before, and the observations will be made on the distances between 400 and 900 yards.

After having been sufficiently drilled in these distances by the detachment so placed, a party composed of a corporal, a bugleman or drummer, and two men fully equipped, will leave the company, and march to some uncertain distance, to be assigned by the instructor as before, by his commanding the party to halt after having passed the distance of 200 yards. The corporal will then place the three men in rank, about a yard asunder, facing the company, and resting on their arms; he will take his position at the right.

The instructor will then cause the exact distance to be measured. During the whole of this operation, the company will be made to face right about, so as to have their backs turned to the party sent forward.

The instructor will then require the officers and non-commissioned officers to compute the distance, each one separately. He will then ascertain from each (without being heard by the others) his computation, and will correct it by informing each of the actual distance.

The officers and non-commissioned officers will then, having made the men face right about, so as to see the party, question each man separately as to his computation of the distance, making each come separately out of the ranks, so as not to be heard by the others. If wrong, they will order him to reconsider the computation, and will note each man's computation on a paper.

So soon as the majority of the company shall have made a computation near the distance, the instructor will order the ground to be again measured before the men. At each distance of 10 yards beyond 200, a signal, to be agreed on, will be given by the bugleman or drummer to the company, and they will be allowed time to appreciate the distance, by observing the measuring party, at the distance at which such party shall then be found.

When this distance shall have been accurately measured, the corporal with his party will advance, and take up a more distant position, with the same precaution of not being seen by the company as before, and the same course of computation of this increased distance, and the same mode of drill will be gone through, as was done for the lesser distance; the men in this case being required to compute, not only the distance from the point first taken up, and the increased distance, but also the whole distance between the company and the increased distance.

These several exercises will be followed out, until the men are capable of accurately computing distances with promptitude,— simply by sight.

There are, however, methods of computing distances by instruments; but which will not in service be generally practicable.

The importance, therefore, of estimating distances by sight cannot be too much insisted on, nor can too much attention be paid to it.

The measuring distances by instruments, is founded on the principle that in proportion to the greater distance, the size of the object is relatively diminished. Thus experience has shewn that at 325 yards, an object has an apparent size of about one-third only of its actual size;—at 435 yards, about one-quarter only;—at 545 yards, about one-fifth only. It may easily be understood then, that if we know the actual height of an object, we may, by comparing its apparent height at any distance unascertained with its real height, arrive at the knowledge of its distance.

Now, suppose we could determine the distance from us of an infantry, or cavalry soldier. The average actual height of an infantry soldier, with his chako, will be about six feet, and that of a mounted trooper, about eight feet; if we then can ascertain his apparent height, we shall, by comparing it with the known diminished height at any given distance, be enabled to ascertain his distance from us. Thus, for instance, we find that the apparent height of an infantry soldier, at some unascertained distance from us, is about two feet, and knowing that at 325 yards, the apparent height of an object is only the one-third of its actual height, and that the actual height of the soldier is six feet, we are enabled to conclude that his distance from us is about 325 yards.

For all practical purposes in Rifle firing this approximation is sufficiently near. We have then to arrive at some means of finding the apparent height of the soldier.

Now to this end, there are various means by the use of instruments ; but as in practice it is necessary to adopt some easy mode, and very extreme precision is not requisite, a rough plan has been adopted of arriving at the desired conclusions.

A rule, having on each side marked the inches, from one inch to three or four feet, and on one side a scale of the distances corresponding to the apparent height of a horseman, and on the other, a similar scale, corresponding to the apparent height of an infantry soldier, is held in the right hand, at arm's length, and in a line with the right eye, and placed vertically or upright, so that the number of inches and the corresponding degree of the scale of distances may be read off. The observer's head being kept perfectly steady and the left eye closed, a sight will be taken, and the upper part of the rule will be applied to the top of the object; for instance, the chako of the infantry soldier; the thumb of the right hand will then be made to slide down the rule, until it comes to the point where another sight being taken, the thumb will appear to be on a level with his feet. The part of the rule between the top and the thumb will then indicate the apparent height of the soldier, and on the corresponding scale will be found the distance.

This is a rough mode of estimation, but will generally be found to be sufficiently accurate for all practical purposes, not exceeding 200 yards distance. This rule may easily be made by any one who may find it necessary.

But there is a more scientific apparatus, called a stadia, which being very simple and easy of application, is generally used.

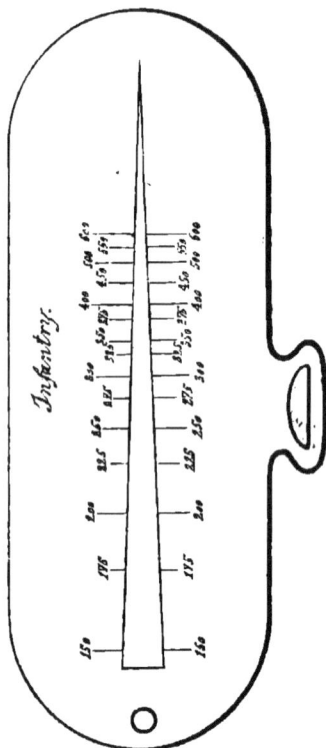

Fig. VIII.

This stadia consists of an isosceles triangle, or a triangle of the form shewn in Fig. VIII., cut out of a piece of thin metal or a card. It will be observed that the interval between the two sides of the triangle diminishes gradually, from the base or bottom, to the summit or top. Taking this base to represent the apparent height of an infantry soldier, at a distance of 200 yards, the different intervals will represent his apparent height at greater distances. A space may therefore be found which will correspond with the apparent height of the soldier at any distance greater than 200 yards, whatever may be that distance. The base and the height of the triangle being chosen, so as not to render the divisions confused, and not inconveniently to multiply the degrees marked on the scale, it will be easy to determine on the triangle the intervals corresponding to certain apparent heights related to 200, 225, 230 yards, and so forth, and this will be sufficiently near for all practical purposes.

The distances are marked with strong or longer lines at 200, 300 yards, &c., and with lighter or shorter lines for intermediate distances, and numbers corresponding to the distances are marked against these lines.

The same instrument may be used, but marked on the reverse side with a different scale, for a cavalry soldier.

When it is desired to use the stadia, to measure for instance the distance of a foot soldier, it is held between the thumb and the two first fingers of the right hand, the base or bottom is held exactly vertical or upright; the arm is held out quite extended in a line with the right eye; the head must be kept perfectly steady, and the left eye be closed. The soldier, whose distance is required, is observed through the triangle, the eye being first directed to bring his head and the top of the upper side of the triangle into one line, and then to bring his feet and the lower side of the triangle also into one, or the lower line, so that the soldier apparently fills the interval of the triangle exactly. The number to denote the corresponding distance is then read off. But if no degree of the scale be exactly opposite to this point, allowance will be made for the difference from the nearest distance.

In using the stadia great care must be taken always to keep it at the same distance from the eye, and to keep the base exactly vertical or upright. Of course it is understood, that where a certain distance is indicated, as that at which the stadia should be held from the eye, this distance must be carefully observed.

In the appreciation of distances necessary for the instruction of troops, the officers and non-commissioned officers may use the stadia.

Beyond 500 yards, the indication of the stadia, from the minute differences in apparent height, cannot be accurately relied on.

In practice, therefore, either these distances must be judged of by estimate, or more perfect instruments, if necessary, must be employed.

Of this description of instrument there are two which have been brought under our notice.

One is the Lunette or Telescope of Messrs. Lerebours and Secretan, * and the other the Telescope or Teleometer of M. Porro, an officer of the Piedmontese Engineers in Italy.

The Lunette of Messrs. Lerebours and Secretan has micrometric wires stretched over the field of the Telescope, as shewn in Fig. V.

Fig. V.

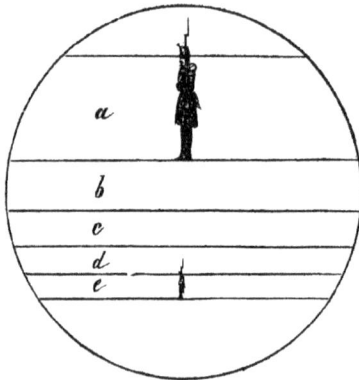

at various distances marked with the letters *a*, *b*, *c*, *d*, and *e*.

The space *a* corresponds to a distance of 200 French metres, or about 110 yards.

The space *b* to about 220 yards.

,,	c	,,	330	,,
,,	d	,,	440	,,
,,	e	,,	550	,,

When a soldier is included between the lines of the space *a*, he is at a distance of about 110 yards. When between the lines of space *b*, about 220 yards, and so on.

If the soldier should not fill more than half of one of these spaces, he is at double the distance indicated by such space. If the half of the height only of the soldier should be included between the lines of any space, he will be at half the distance indicated by such space.

---

* The eminent Opticians of the French Imperial Observatory and Marine, 13, Place du Pont Neuf, Paris.

The height of a soldier is here measured from the soles of his feet to the line of his eyes.

The Prismatic Micrometric Telescope or Teleometer of Monsieur Porro, derives its name of Teleometer, from two Greek words, signifying "a measurer of distances." By a happy adaptation of prisms, as reflectors, its length is reduced from the ordinary dimension to about the measure of the breadth of the hand (Fig. VII.), so as to be easily portable, and it is set for any eye in a moment, by a small screw moved by the thumb.

Fig. VII.

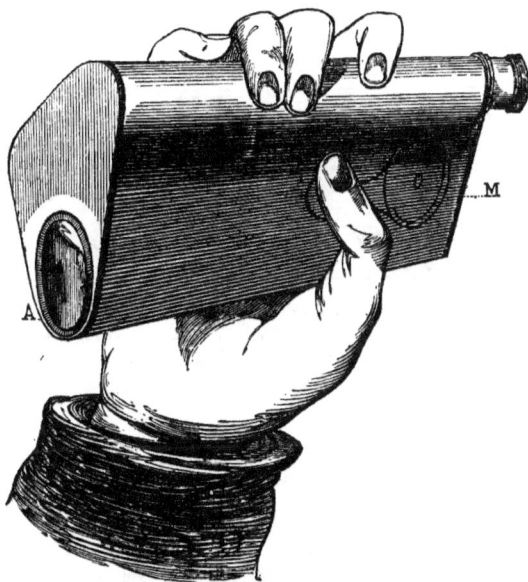

Our limits will not allow us to describe particularly the optical arrangements of this instrument, which would lead us away from our present subject into too lengthened and too scientific details on the principles and effects of reflection; we must content ourselves by stating, that it may be used either as an ordinary telescope, or as a means of measuring the distance from the eye, of any object whose actual height is known. It is in this latter application that we shall now particularly consider the teleometer of M. Porro.

An apparatus is adapted to a small tube, which contains the focal glass, or that glass which is applied to the eye, consisting of wires stretched across this tube at various spaces, such as that shewn in Fig. VI., Fig. 1, Fig. 2, Fig. 3.

Fig. VI.

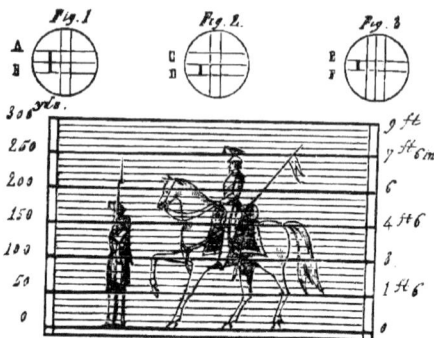

The Prismatic Teleometer, or Micrometric Telescope.

By the subdivisions of the scale at the side, the whole, or a part only, of the object, whose total height is known, may be taken as a term of comparison in the estimation of distances. The object or part of the object selected must correspond exactly with one of the spaces, or in other words, be intercepted by two of the wires of the Teleometer.

The Micrometer is an apparatus applied to the focal glass of the Telescope; it consists of five wires placed across the disc of the telescope, as shewn in Figs. 1, 2, 3, in which A B shews one space; C D a second; and E F a third space. A B shews the distance to be equal to 100 times the height of the object; C D 200 times; and E F 500 times.

1st Example.—If the lower wire of the space A B cuts or crosses the knees of a body of infantry, the other line the points of the bayonets, the scale on the left hand gives 200 yards distance.

2nd Example.—If one of the wires of the space C D touches the feet, the other the waistband of an infantry soldier, the scale would give 110 double yards, or 220 yards distance.

3rd Example.—If one of the wires of the space E F cuts or crosses the horse's hoofs, the other the epaulettes of the cavalry soldier, the scale will give 250 times 5 yards, or 1,250 yards.

These wires have three separate spaces, viz., A B, including the space occupied by three wires, or in other words, between the upper and lower wire; C D, the space between two wires,—the intermediate and lower wire; and E F, the space between two other wires, not so distant from each other as C D.

Now these spaces, A B, C D, and E F, represent three distinct distances from the eye; the first, or A B, 100 times as great; the second, or C D, 200 times as great; and the third, or E F, 500 times as great, as the actual height of an object looked at through the teleometer.

On the diagram or plan, (Fig. VI.,) a scale will be found applied to the actual heights of an infantry and a cavalry soldier. On the right hand are the figures 0, 1 ft. 6 in., 3 ft., 4 ft. 6 in., or scale of heights up to 9 ft. or 3 yards. Between these figures are lines running from the left to the right, or horizontally, dividing each yard into tenth parts, for the facility of calculation; by examining these figures and lines, the height of an infantry soldier is found to be given as about 6 feet or 2 yards, and that of a cavalry soldier and his horse, as about 8 feet.

On the left or opposite side of the scale, are figures ranging from 0 to 300. These figures denote the distance of the object, as measured by A B. The intervals between the figures on the scale are again subdivided into fifths, by the horizontal lines running from left to right.

Now it will be remembered that the space between the wires A B, (*Fig. I.*) shews an object to be at a distance equal to 100 times its actual height, when the object is included between them; C D, 200 times; and E F, 500 times the actual height.

We will now shew how this instrument is used to measure distances.

First example: Let the lower line of the space A B cut or cross the knees of an infantry soldier who is at a distance, and let the upper line cut or cross the point of his bayonet; on looking to the figures on the right of the scale, we find that the actual height of this part of the man with his bayonet, is 2 yards. Now since the figures on the left indicate the distance, we find the space between 50, (the line of the knees on the scale,) and 250, (the line of the bayonet,) to be 200; and as the quantity is taken in yards, we find therefore the scale to indicate that the soldier is at 200 yards distance.

This scale, therefore, corresponds with the indications of A B, taken in another point of view. We have seen that the space A B has shewn the height by the scale to be 2 yards, and as this space shews an object at 100 times the distance from the eye, we multiply 2 yards by 100, which gives us 200 yards, the actual distance of the object.

Again, as another example: Let us take the space E F, (*Fig.* 3) and apply it to a cavalry soldier. We find that from the feet of the horse to the head of the rider, is included within E F. Now on the right hand of the scale we find that the actual height of him and his horse to this point, is $2\frac{1}{2}$ yards; we therefore multiply 2½ yards by 500, and we find 1,250 yards to be the distance from the object.

This result is not shewn in figures on the left hand of the scale, which, to avoid confusion, is confined to the distances shewn by A B, but it could be easy to add them for C D and E F, and they may be ascertained by multiplying the distances on the scale by 2 and 5 respectively.

It is most important that soldiers should be accustomed to judge of distances correctly; that they should know how far their Rifles will carry point-blank; and also the exact degree of elevation that is required, in order to hit objects at different distances beyond that point-blank range. They should therefore be trained to a knowledge of distances on every kind of ground, and be at all times prepared to answer correctly the following simple questions:—

Firstly, What is the point-blank range of your Rifle?

Secondly, Does it carry to the right or left?

Thirdly, How many yards are you distant from such an object?

Fourthly, What is the requisite degree of elevation in order to enable you to hit the body of a man at 200, 250, 300 yards, &c., and so on.

There is another essential point connected with distances, to which it is necessary to direct particular attention, which is the firing at an object in motion.

A foot soldier gets over in a minute at quick march about 72 yards, at the pace of a charge about 88 yards. A horse walks over about 433 yards in 4½ minutes, trots over the same distance in about two minutes, and gallops over the same distance in about one minute.

A foot soldier occupies in rank a width of about 2 feet; a trooper about 3 feet.

Now suppose that a cavalry soldier be moving to or from the point of the line of vision, which is at point-blank range; it is clear that if the Rifle be fired to strike at point-blank range, the ball will either fall short of, or go beyond the cavalry soldier by the distance that will be passed by him, during the time taken in the flight of the ball. Allowance must therefore in such circumstances be made for this distance.

Suppose him to be coming nearer, in a direction perpendicular to the plane of projection, and to be at the point of point-blank range when aimed at. Allowance must be made for his being somewhat nearer when the ball shall reach him, and an aim must be taken accordingly below the line of vision, or in other words, at the feet of the horse. By such means, as the ball rises in the trajectory, within point-blank range, the ball would strike the head of the horse or the rider.

Suppose on the other hand, the cavalry soldier be riding away · in the same plane of projection, allowance must be made for his being more distant when the ball reaches him, and an aim must then be taken above the line of vision, or in other words, at the head of the cavalry soldier ; and since, as the trajectory falls below the point-blank range after it has passed it, the ball would strike the body of the horse, or the rider, in such case.

Allowance must also be made in case of his moving to the right or to the left; but as in this case his distance would be nearly the same, it will only be necessary to direct the Rifle to the right or left, so as to compensate the probable distance in either of such directions that he may pass over.

In being engaged with an enemy, it will always be desirable in estimating the distance, to fire the first round rather before than beyond him, since this will lead to a more just appreciation of the distance than could be obtained by firing beyond him; besides which, there would be the chance that the fire would not be thrown away, since the ricochet or bound of the balls may do him as serious an injury as a fire directed exactly into his ranks.

The just appreciation of distance is, we repeat, of the highest importance. Well skilled in this, the soldier seldom throws away a shot, and this has a double effect,—the saving his ammunition, and the intimidating and destroying his enemy. The value of his ammunition can never be too highly estimated, since nothing inspires more confidence in him than that he has a cartouch box well provided against every emergency. One single charge of ammunition may be the means, under a variety of circumstances, of saving his life, or of turning the tide of victory in his favour. The effect, too, of a well directed fire on an enemy is not confined simply to his destruction, it distracts him, and throws him into disorder, and nothing makes so strong an impression on him, as the having his ranks thinned by every discharge, whilst on the other hand it tends to animate and encourage the troops who are opposed to the enemy, and opens to them the chances of victory ; not only by the cutting up the enemy's ranks, but by introducing among them that fear of the skill and coolness of their opponents, which has a great moral influence in favour of the latter. Nothing, moreover, affords so favourable an opportunity for a successful charge, as the effects produced by a steady and well directed fire. On the other hand, a hasty and ill-directed fire, leads an enemy to hold his opponents in contempt, and creates in him such confidence, as once felt, seldom quits him during the combat.

CHAPTER V.

CAUSES OF DEVIATION IN THE FIRING, AND THEIR REMEDIES.

THERE are several causes which may produce a failure, or imperfection in firing.

First. Because of ignorance of the principles of firing, and the necessary management of the Rifle.

Secondly. Because the ball may, and generally does, suffer deviations from the leaving the Rifle in its passage through the air.

The first class of causes may be materially, if not wholly obviated, by the attention given to the instructor, and practice of the men.

The second class of causes depends on the quality of the Rifle, and on exterior influences operating on the ball. The most expert marksman, and most skilful shot, cannot obviate some of these causes.

The principles we have laid down, as to taking aim, must be applied with reference to these causes.

The Rifles are not always of the same make, nor is the make always regular and perfect, as we have been compelled to assume it to be, in laying down general principles.

Sometimes, for instance, the line of vision of the Rifle itself is not exactly in the same plane with the axis of the barrel. It happens, therefore, that an aim taken with the sight and back sight, would not carry the ball in the plane of the true line of vision. In this case, therefore, the defect in the Rifle being ascertained, aim must be taken to the right or left, according as the true line of vision is to the right or left of the plane of projection of the Rifle. The distance to be taken to the right or left, must depend on the imperfection of the Rifle, and on the distance of the object, a corresponding greater allowance being made for a corresponding greater distance. This, however, is an imperfection that will not generally be found in the Rifle to any great extent.

Not only may this defect of the Rifle, in popular language

carrying to the right or to the left, exist, but the sights may be found not accurately to correspond with the distances marked. This is a much more common defect, and one very difficult to be avoided. If it depended simply on the imperfection of the sight and back sights, it might be corrected without much difficulty, but its principal cause is the difference in the calibre, or bore of the Rifle, which, though in some cases being almost inappreciable, still exercises very considerable influence, and would require that the sights of each Rifle should be mathematically adjusted to suit the calibre or bore.

Every soldier must, therefore, observe very carefully the effects produced by his Rifle, and make a compensation accordingly.

Another cause of deviation in the length of the range, will be found in the difference of cartridges; since with what care soever they may be manufactured, differences will exist when made on a large scale, either in the quality or quantity of the powder, or in other respects.

Another cause of deviation, is the Rifle being held not in the plane of the line of vision, but inclined to the right or to the left; these effects are the more apparent as the inclination is greater, and the distance of the object is increased : and, therefore, the greater the distance of the object, the greater the necessity of avoiding this cause of deviation.

Another cause of deviation, and which we must again press on our hearers, is the change of direction occasioned by pulling the trigger, especially if it pull hard. To obviate this, we must again propose the necessity of constant practice.

Of the causes of deviation arising from external influences, may be noticed,—the wind, the temperature, and the humidity or dampness and density of the atmosphere ; the position of the sun, and the difference of level between the object and the Rifle.

First. The wind.

When the wind is opposite to the direction of the ball, the ball finds a greater resistance than in a calm atmosphere, and is proportionally lowered.

When the wind is in the same direction as the ball, it increases the velocity of the ball, and the ball is raised in the plane of projection.

When the wind forms an angle with the line of the ball, or in common language, blows from either side, the ball is carried to the side opposite to the wind ; and the more so, as the wind is at right angles, and as the force of the wind is great, and as in the other cases already mentioned, the greater the distance of the object, the greater the deviation.

Secondly. The temperature, humidity or dampness, and density of the atmosphere.

These have an effect on the ball, and occasion deviations in its course. When the temperature is high, the density of the atmosphere is generally less, and the ball will rise, but still in the plane of projection; a contrary effect takes place at low temperatures, attended with increased density, or with humidity of the atmosphere. Generally in dry weather, the range is somewhat longer.

Thirdly. The position of the sun will materially operate, by deceiving the soldier as to the real place of the points, which determine the line of vision.

When the sun is to the right, the right part of the sight is lighted, while the left is in shadow; a bright spot is also seen on the right side of the sight, which will attract the attention of the man, and which will lead him to think the middle of the sight nearer to the right than it really is; a contrary effect is produced when the sun is on the left side. The soldier is thus led to direct the line of vision out of the direct line.

This error is to be avoided by directing the aim a little to the right, when the sun is on the right side; and a little to the left, when the sun is on the left side.

Fourthly. In giving rules for firing in our former Lectures, we have supposed the line of vision to be horizontal, or deviating but little from a horizontal line.

When the positions of the object, and the party firing, are not on the same level, the form of the trajectory changes; and if, in such case, the usual rules are followed scrupulously, the object will not be struck.

When the line of vision is above the horizon, the trajectory is less curved, and when below the horizon, it is more curved.

When an object, therefore, is placed on an elevation, aim must be taken above the object, and when it is on ground lower than the horizon, aim must be taken below it.

The foulness of the Rifle is also another cause of deviation.

The heating a Rifle, by long continued firing, also creates deviation. As the Rifle becomes more heated, the ball will have a tendency to rise, and for this, allowance must be made.

The injury to the cartridges from having been a long time in the cartridge pouch; from their being shaken and injured on a long march; from the powder becoming damp from the humidity of the atmosphere, rain, or other cause, are also reasons of deviation, which must be particularly attended to.

In wet weather, the soldier must be very careful to prevent the rain getting into the barrel, lock, or nipple of his Rifle, which would have a material effect in causing a deviation, if not of wholly rendering useless his Rifle.

CHAPTER VI.

GENERAL OBSERVATIONS.

TO give the soldier facility and skill in the art of Rifle firing in as short a time, and with as little useless expenditure of ammunition as may be, by teaching him the principles and explaining the practice of taking correct aim and firing, and the means of accurately estimating distances, has been the object of the former part of this treatise.

On the utility of exercises in firing by the infantry, much difference of opinion has hitherto prevailed; but with our present means, we may well, I think, consider the time to have gone by, when it was asserted that not one ball in 1500 did any damage to an enemy, and that in some campaigns every dead man cost his weight in lead. The want of address of the soldier has been often considered an evil without remedy, Whence has arisen this opinion? The American, the Corsican, the Algerine, the riflemen of the Tyrol, even the Caffre, have performed extraordinary feats of dexterity. And what is to prevent the British infantry soldier with a Rifle of equal or nearly equal excellence, from coming within something like an approachable distance of them? Nothing, but the absence of a knowledge of principles, and a want of practice, and the not having the coolness and self-possession before an enemy, which are felt under ordinary circumstances.

To remedy the former branch of this deficiency, has been the end we have had in view in this essay. As a means of obviating the latter, we must address ourselves to the intelligence and well known moral courage of our soldiers. Nothing is so important in the field as coolness and steadiness. And whence are these derived ? From a confidence by troops that their arms are efficient; that their skill in the use of them is unquestionable ; and a conviction that they are doing their duty.

We know that any appeal to the courage of our men is unnecessary; all that is required of us, is only so to direct it, that it may not be exerted in vain. With this view, we are confident that we have only to point out to them the great advantages that must result from no haste or precipitancy in firing; from the coolly and deliberately taking aim ; from so far as possible acting in no more hurried manner, than if no enemy were before them ; and from economising their ammunition, and not throwing away a single shot.

Haste and precipitancy are frequently productive of ill results; yet in few situations may they be more so, than in a field of battle. Rapid firing, combined with skill, may be sometimes useful and even necessary ; but rapidity without skill is worse, infinitely worse than useless. It is mischievous, nay dangerous; mischievous, in that it does not harm an enemy, and gives him confidence by creating a contempt for his opponents, while it begets a corresponding want of confidence in one's comrades ;—and dangerous, in that it uselessly expends that ammunition, the due economy of which should be one of a soldier's first cares, and deprives him of it without cause, when it might have been husbanded for a juncture, in which the having it might save the soldier's life. The soldier should have this truth impressed firmly on his mind, *that it is better to fire one shot with effect in ten minutes, than to fire ten ineffectual shots in one minute.* It does more execution, and does not waste ammunition.

The fire of the infantry must have, in all future warfare, an immense influence in the fate of battles, and it is to the rendering this as perfect as may be, that our present efforts are directed.

To instruct a man who has passed some twenty years of his life unaccustomed to the use of fire-arms, is doubtless a difficulty; but a difficulty that, with adequate information and zealous practice, may be so surmounted as to make him nearly as efficient as any of the men of whose prowess some extraordinary facts are extant.

We are of opinion that the firing with ball is by no means essential in practice, to the making an expert marksman, and

O

it is with this conviction that we would press on instructors, on the one hand, to devote most of their attention to the preliminary exercises recommended in our first chapter, of practising aiming, and the management of the Rifle in firing, including particularly the steadily pulling the trigger, so as not thereby to change the position of the Rifle; and, on the other hand, would press on recruits to submit patiently and cheerfully to such preliminary exercises, as a certain means of making them skilful shots, and thus affording them the many great advantages which result.

In the firing with ball, it is almost wholly impossible to make the necessary corrections in the position of the Rifle, the correctness of aim, the proper elevation, the steadiness of the Rifle, or the mode of pulling the trigger ; all essential to a good marksman, and inaccuracy in any one of which, will cause ammunition to be thrown away.   Errors may exist in all these, and yet at the moment of firing, hazard may direct the ball to the bull's eye, whereas if due attention be paid to, and sufficient practice be had in, these preliminary exercises, under careful inspection and correction, the shot will never be one of hazard, but will always be certain, as the result of skill.

The effect on the recruit too, of allowing him to fire ball before he has acquired sufficient dexterity to be assured of his mark, will tend to make him a sort of chance shot. He fires, and his ball has gone to the left ; he tries again, the same causes produce similar effects. He now finds his ball has gone to the right ; he fires too high, and to remedy this, he now fires too low.   He is quite bewildered, and at length comes to the conclusion that his Rifle is faulty, or discovers some other cause, but not that it is want of skill, arising, in great measure, from his having been made to fire ball at a mark, without having had the necessary preliminary instruction and practice, to fit him for certainty and success.   The result of all this is, that every soldier fires after his own fashion, and that, without the possibility of any other correction from those who superintend him, than simply that his ball has failed in this or that manner.

There is another point, and that, too, of no little importance in adopting principally these preliminary exercises,—they are attended with no expenditure of ammunition, and may consequently be used every day ; while ball firing, from its cost, can only be occasionally resorted to, so that the soldier may have a hundred days' practice in the one, for one day's practice in the other.   Of the consequence there can be little doubt.

In these preliminary exercises, the end of which is to make the men expert shots, it may be as well, so far as possible, for the superintending officer or instructor to avoid giving the word of command; since the soldier, accustomed to discipline and prompt obedience, may frequently pay more attention to the immediate execution of the command, than to correct aiming, or the management of his Rifle in firing.

While on the subject of these preliminary exercises, it may be well—by way of impressing on the minds of the instructor and soldier, a point of very high importance, the pulling the trigger so as not to cause any change in the position of the Rifle—to recur to that subject, and notice it a little more in detail, than we found it necessary to do in our first chapter.

It is not difficult to keep the Rifle steady in the direction of the object aimed at, so long as there is no motion in pulling the trigger; but this movement creates at once a difficulty. The pressure on the trigger throws the Rifle generally to the right, especially if the spring of the lock be hard. As some means of compensating this, aim should in most cases be taken, therefore, rather to the left than to the right part of an object.

This, however, is not all that is requisite. The man must carefully keep his Rifle to the aim, during all the time that he is pulling the trigger, and he must pull the trigger by a steady and continued pressure of the finger, without the slightest jerk or irregularity, and so, that he may be almost unaware of the identical moment at which the Rifle will go off; and during the whole of this time he must suspend or stop his breathing. The trigger, it will be remembered, is to be pulled with the second joint of the first finger, and as this is a matter of the very greatest importance, it may be as well for the instructor himself particularly to shew each man separately the manner in which this is to be done.

The men, after having pulled the trigger, should still continue to hold the Rifle in the line of aim, and observe whether it has changed its position. And the whole of this exercise should be repeated until they have attained a perfect steadiness in position before, during, and after the fire.

In taking aim, the left eye being shut, the right eye is to be fixed stedfastly on the object, or rather on that part of it to which the aim should be particularly directed; and the Rifle should be raised gradually until it is accurately in line. Experience has shewn, that to *strike an object it is necessary to see it distinctly at the moment of firing.*

There are certain particular rules with reference to taking aim, that we have reserved for this place.

When an object of a certain size is fired at, at point-blank range, the centre of the object is the point to be aimed at, for if any of the extremities be taken, there will be greater chance of missing it, by a deviation of the ball, or by inaccuracy of aim.

If aim on either side the centre be taken, it would always be preferable that it should be rather to the left than to the right, to compensate, as was just now observed, for any change of position caused by pulling the trigger.

The first fixed sight on the Rifle is for distances of 200 yards, and the second fixed sight for 400 yards.

If the object be at less than 300 or 400 yards, the lower part of it must be aimed at, because, as we have shewn in our first chapter, the trajectory (as seen in Figs. I., II., III.,) rises above the line of vision, for all points within the point-blank range.

If the object be exactly at 200 or 400 yards, the centre of the object must be aimed at, because the trajectory cuts or directly meets the line of vision at point-blank range.   If the object be beyond 200 or 400 yards, the upper part of the object must be aimed at, because beyond the point-blank range, the trajectory falls below the line of vision.

This rule, of course, has reference to distances within about twenty-five or thirty yards, on either side of point-blank range ; since, if the distance be greater, a corresponding allowance of elevation or depression in the aim must be made.

For distances beyond 400 yards, the movable bar or slide of the sight may be adapted, very nearly to the actual distance ; but it must be borne in mind, that at all intermediate distances at which the movable slide will not exactly indicate the distance, allowance must be made for the difference, by elevating or raising the aim, if the object be beyond point-blank range, and by depressing or lowering the aim, if it be at less than point-blank range.

All this will be readily seen and understood by looking at the diagram or plan (Fig. II.) of the line of vision and the trajectory.

To illustrate these rules practically, it would be well to have a series of targets (as in Fig. IV.) placed at stated distances in the same horizontal line, the bull's eyes being all placed also in a horizontal line, by which means the soldier may be shewn the effect of every shot.

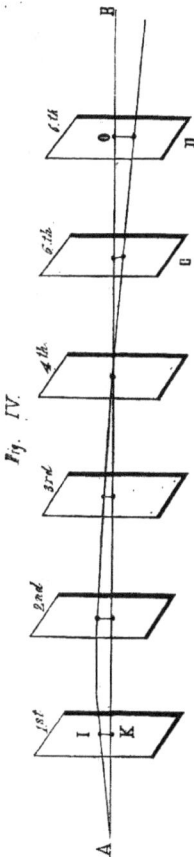

These targets may be numbered from 1 to 6. The target No. 4, should be placed exactly at point-blank range, and the other targets, being at certain known distances, say at ten yards apart, the target No. 1 would be thirty yards before or within the point-blank range, and the target No. 6, twenty yards behind or without the point-blank range. The soldier may then be directed so to adjust his aim, that his ball shall strike an object at thirty, twenty, or ten yards within point-blank range, at point-blank range, or at ten or twenty yards without, or beyond point-blank range. The target No. 4 not being seen by him, it is clear that he cannot, by firing at the object which is exactly at point-blank range, attain as a necessary consequence the trajectory in the other targets, and he will therefore be compelled to adjust his aim so as to strike the object he is required to do.

The position of these targets may be varied from time to time, so as to shew the trajectory in any required relation to the point-blank range, and thus may the soldier be taught practically, and pretty correctly, the curve of the trajectory,—both within, or before—and without, or beyond point-blank range; a knowledge of great importance to him, especially when firing at an object in motion.

These and similar important rules it would be well to have printed and circulated among the troops for their private and special study.

We now come to another point. There are several positions that may be taken by the soldier in firing :—

First. An upright or standing position.

Secondly. On his knee.

Thirdly. Lying down in any position.

Little need be said on the first position, since the exercises will be principally in this position, and attention to the rules we have already prescribed will render the soldier sufficiently competent in this.

As to the second, the position on the knee, much difference of opinion exists as to its advantage, among very competent authorities; some of them considering it generally to be avoided, as much as may be, from its not being military; from its affecting the accuracy of the fire; and from the loss of time occasioned in loading, from the necessity of rising to an upright position for loading, and returning again to the same·position for firing. It has therefore been recommended that in practice it should be used but seldom.

On this point, we would, however, bring under the reader's notice, and submit to the consideration of instructors, the remarks made by a very high French authority in an elaborate work on firing with portable arms. He says :

" It is incontestable that when the soldier is in some sort
" left to himself, when he is out of the ranks, in a word, when
" employed as a sharp-shooter, that his skill, as a marksman,
" produces its best effect. Ought he in such situation to be
" compelled to take this or that position? Certainly not!
" The man places himself as he finds best, and takes the
" position most convenient to him. For the great majority
" of men, the position on the knee is preferable, as to steadiness
" and firmness, to the upright position ; it allows him to aim
" more certainly, and fatigues the left arm much less, by the
" support afforded to the elbow by the knee, and is almost
" sure to produce shots of more effect. A well-practised
" soldier will easily take and quit this position ; besides, it has
" this advantage, that it only exposes half the surface to the
" fire of an enemy. It cannot be termed unmilitary, since the
" front rank is frequently obliged to take this position.

" We are therefore far from thinking that this position
" should be exceptional; we think it should be particularly
" attended to, and more especially where men are likely to
" be employed in detached bodies, or singly; and we. are
" quite sure that we have with us the opinion of all the officers
" who are generally employed as instructors in firing, when
" we say that it is the position *par excellence* for every man
" whom it is desired to make a finished marksman."

The third class of positions requires from us no particular notice here.

We have, throughout this treatise, used the term "Rifle," and some portion of it has particular and exclusive reference to that weapon. We have confined ourselves to this term, "Rifle," to avoid unnecessary repetition and confusion; but, as will readily be understood by the intelligent reader, the greater part of our essay will equally apply to the Musket, or any other portable fire-arm, that may be employed. There is, however, one cause of deviation in the musket, which does not exist in the Rifle. For the musket, the ball is cast somewhat smaller than the bore, and leaves, therefore, a space between its surface and the barrel, when it is rammed down. This space is called "windage." Now, if the ball be not, as it very seldom is, placed exactly in the centre of the barrel, the powder exploding in this windage, as well as below the ball, occasions a deviation in the ball, and not only so, but makes sometimes a marked difference in the range.

On this, and many other accounts, it is impossible to fire with a musket, with the same precision as a Rifle. Much, however, of this difference, may be compensated by care being taken in the loading.

The principal difference between the Rifle and the infantry musket, lies in the difference between the ranges. Experience has shewn that the point-blank range of the musket is about 100 yards.

In the same manner as in the case of the Rifle, the trajectory rises above the line of vision, within, or short of this range, and falls below it, without, or beyond the point-blank range.

In order, therefore, to strike an object at less than 100 yards, the aim must be taken below the line of vision. At 100 yards, it must be taken at the object; and above 100 yards, the aim must be taken above the object, in the proportion in which the trajectory lies above or below the line of vision.

To reduce this to practical rule, we will suppose the object to be struck, to be an infantry soldier :—

> At 125 yards and any shorter distance near to it, aim at the centre of the soldier.
> At 150 yards aim at his breast.
> At 175 yards aim at his head.
> At 200 yards aim at the top of the chako.
> Beyond 200 yards, there is no point within the limits of the man, at which aim can be taken with a common musket.

Suppose, again, that the object to be struck is a cavalry soldier.

> At 125 yards, or a little less, aim must be taken, with the musket, at the horse's chest.
> At 150 yards, at his head.
> At 175 yards, at the breast of the rider.
> At 200 yards, at the rider's head.
> At 225 yards, at the top of his helmet.

There is one other point to which we must advert, before concluding our Treatise, and which, though apparently of minor importance, may yet have important effects in retarding the progress of some of the younger recruits; and this is the recoil, or kick of the firelock. This may arise, either from an excessive charge, or from the piece not being held firmly pressed to the shoulder at the moment of firing.

The latter cause is the only probable one in the army, since the cartridges are all adapted as a proper charge to the Rifle or musket. The remedy, therefore, for the recoil, or kick, lies with the soldier himself; and, independently of avoiding all recoil, the holding firmly the musket to the shoulder has another essential advantage, the tending to keep steady the musket in firing.

Sometimes, with every care and precaution, a musket may miss fire. In this case it should still be held to the shoulder, until all chance of its going off has ceased; since, not unfrequently, it may hang fire for several seconds, and if removed too soon, might cause an accident to the man or his comrades. A skilful and steady shot may always be recognized by his attention to this precaution.

If a musket should miss fire, care should also be taken in pricking or cleaning the nipple, to direct the muzzle away from any one, as it often happens that a portion of the percussion powder is left on the nipple, and will, by friction in cleaning, cause the charge to explode.

Such are the general directions, within the limits of which will be found what is essential for a soldier to observe in this branch of his duty. We may add to this, that if it should be his fortune to be called into the field to meet his country's foes, great care must be taken by him in firing, that it be not hurried, and that he present deliberately; bring up his firelock gradually; and look stedfastly at his object before he fires,—otherwise his fire will lose all its effect upon the enemy. The value of his ammunition must be highly estimated by him, and the most extreme jealousy of its expenditure must be entertained. In proportion as a cool and well-directed fire serves to distract and throw an enemy into disorder, so a wild, confused, and hurried fire (which is always without effect,) is calculated to give him confidence, and a contempt for his opponent. It is impossible therefore to labour too much to give to soldiers the habit of steady, cool, and effective firing. They should bear in mind, that nothing makes so strong an impression upon an enemy, as the thinning his ranks by a well-directed fire, and that nothing tends to animate and encourage troops more than the diminished fire from ranks so thinned; and besides this, it affords the best chance of adopting that,—in which the British soldier has won so many laurels,—"a successful charge."

It has been said, that you never can place British troops too near an enemy, and in a figurative sense, as descriptive of courage and daring, this is still as true as ever; but as a matter of military science, and a means of obtaining victory with the least expenditure of human life, which is the end of every wise and humane commander, the being able to place troops at distances at which they will be less exposed to destruction, except by skill, tends to render warfare more scientific, and, therefore, less generally sanguinary.

In this view, we cannot but consider the Rifle, like every other invention in warlike weapons, which are more destructive than those by which they have been preceded, as a valuable addition to our military implements; and although it may oblige us to keep at a more respectful distance from our enemies, than has heretofore been our custom, yet there can be no doubt that that will be far from being a reason against our giving a good account of them, should we be called on to prove that we are now as efficient with the Rifle, as we have shewn ourselves heretofore with the musket. We hope that the necessity of this may not arise, but if it should, we know the British soldier will do his duty.